Waiting in Joyful Hope

Daily Reflections for
Advent and Christmas
2018–2019

Genevieve Glen

LITURGICAL PRESS

Collegeville, Minnesota

www.litpress.org

Nihil Obstat: Reverend Robert Harren, J.C.L., *Censor deputatus.*
Imprimatur: ✠ Most Reverend Donald J. Kettler, J.C.L., Bishop of Saint Cloud, March 8, 2018.

Cover design by Monica Bokinskie. Cover art courtesy of Getty Images.

ISSN: 1550-803X
ISBN: 978-0-8146-4496-6   978-0-8146-4535-2 (ebook)

Introduction

Advent and Christmas together form the season of the gift anticipated, celebrated, and passed on.

Remember, though, that gifts from the God of surprises are never predictable. Unlike Santa's, God's gift to you might not come on time. Quite likely it won't be wrapped neatly. And it probably won't look like the one you were expecting. The opening sentence above ties Advent and Christmas up neatly in fairly traditional ribbons, but as soon as the first Advent hymn is sung on Sunday, December 2, they will start to come untied.

The reason is that this unpredictable gift is not simply the Christ Child whose birth we celebrate on December 25. The gift is the life that comes to us in and through Christ still living among us as God's love made human flesh. Advent invites us to look forward to this newness of life, but it also warns us that God's plan for our lives may not coincide with our own! Israel sometimes yearned for a new warrior king who would save the nation from oppression and restore the Davidic kingdom to its former glory. Instead, Jesus brought the new peaceful reign of God bristling with totally different gifts and challenges. We see the same unexpectedness at work in the lives of key Advent figures, like Mary and Joseph, John the Baptist—and even Herod!

We celebrate the memory of this always-startling Savior's birth on December 25, but God is notoriously bad about obeying calendars, mere human foibles that they are. You may wake up on December 10 to new snow on the ground and new life in your heart, perhaps caused by God's gift of a phone call from an estranged child asking the family's forgiveness and an invitation to Christmas dinner. Or you may suffer through a crazy Christmas full of conflict, only to meet Christ deeply and personally as the source of your peace on New Year's Day, the World Day of Prayer for Peace. (God does *sometimes* honor calendars!)

Whenever the gift of renewed life in Christ arrives and however it's packaged, it comes with an instruction manual. Unlike the user's manual for your new phone or the assembly instructions for your new towel rack, this instruction book is not written in the alien language of technology or the impossible syntax of a bad translation. It's written clearly in the language of human experience beyond Christmas, like the hint about what to do with holiday leftovers on January 8 or the push into Ordinary Time work on January 13. The new life we receive in Christ is given to be lived, as his was and is, to build up the reign of God by handing on the gift of love to other people.

We celebrate Advent and Christmas every year. But remember Christ's promise: "Behold, I make all things new" (Rev 21:5). Whatever past gifts were, this year's will be different. Wait for them—with joyful hope!

FIRST WEEK OF ADVENT

Be Not Afraid!

Readings: Jer 33:14-16; 1 Thess 3:12–4:2; Luke 21:25-28, 34-36

Scripture:
People will die of fright
in anticipation of what is coming upon the world. . . .
And then they will see the Son of Man
coming in a cloud with power and great glory.
But when these signs begin to happen,
stand erect and raise your heads
because your redemption is at hand. (Luke 21:26-27)

Reflection: The daily news has trained us well in disaster thinking: arctic ice melt will flood New York, terrorist attacks lurk in crowded malls, earthquakes and sinkholes threaten, and nuclear weapons are proliferating in unfriendly places. The chief strategy for survival remains what it has been since biblical times: run! hide! My generation built back-yard bomb shelters fully equipped for an unbearable future. In 2017, Stephen Hawking began urging the whole human race to pack our bags, turn out the lights, and find a new planet—soon!

No wonder the gospel reports of cosmic upheavals preced-ing Christ's return in a glory-lit cloud sometimes scare believers! However, despite the predictions, this is not a nuclear landfall we're expecting. Christ's final advent is no disaster! The gospel "signs" actually paint a vivid picture of the new creation coming to birth, echoing Genesis 1. Yes, it will bring changes as the creative breath of God blows us out of our familiar comfort zones into a new world. And change is frightening. Isn't there an easier solution? Couldn't God just spiff up the world as we know it, calm it down a little, repair some of the cracks, make us better tenants? Probably—but God's love wants a far better future for us than we dare to want for ourselves. A brand-new creation, all the scars of sin and death erased, is the least of God's plans. Profound communion in love with God, one another, and all things comes closer to describing the future we dare not imagine, but God has.

And that future began long ago, when the Word of God took out full membership in humanity and our story. We remember Christ's first coming with joyful festivity, though it initiated life changes we still find hard. He has promised to return in the end, bringing with him all the holy ones—our own loved ones included. Do we really want to slam the bomb shelter doors shut and hope for a return to the sinful, polluted, violent world we call normal?

Instead, says Jesus, stand up and raise your heads! Redemption, not catastrophe, is coming. Ignore the recitals of doom. We sing a different song: "O come, O come, Emmanuel!"

Meditation: Do you fear the changes Christ brings, even now? What might you lose? Don't let dread drown out his words: "Fear not! It is I!"

Prayer: Come, Lord Jesus!

Lost in the Dark

Readings: Isa 2:1-5; Matt 8:5-11

Scripture:
O house of Jacob, come,
let us walk in the light of the LORD! (Isa 2:5)

Reflection: Two of us were on the highway between the local town and our rural monastery. The sun disappeared behind the mountains while errands and appointments kept us late in the well-lit safety of familiar stores and gas stations and neighborhoods. But we left the streetlights, and the safety, behind when we drove north out of town toward home. As the road climbed toward the monastery, we remembered all too vividly the rocks in the ravines we could no longer see beside the highway. In places, the day's leftover snow had turned into patches of ice, now invisible. There are no streetlights on the road to our monastery. We searched urgently for the one light that marks the entrance to our valley. Without it, we were lost in the dark, no longer sure of the way home.

As the December nights lengthen, the holiday lights brighten and threaten to blind us. They flash insistent expectations: get to the office party next week—the boss expects it; get the latest electronic toys for your children—they expect it; stretch that slim budget to provide for the traditional meal, and invite everyone—your family or friends expect it. We feel lost amid the chaos of demands and look desperately for the light at the gate that will somehow take us home, even though we may be unsure about where home is.

The prophet Isaiah calls out in our darkness, "Come . . . walk in the light of the LORD!" That's not a streetlamp. That's a person: Jesus Christ is the Light of the World, and our pathfinder.

God keeps that light on in the window of our real home and is always out looking for those who have missed it. And God has very good hearing. Whisper "Come, Christ our Light" in any situation, and Christ will be there shining the lamp for your feet, the light for your path (see Ps 119:105).

Meditation: Think about the holiday demands that stress you the most. Picture them as flashing lights. Try to close your eyes to them by imagining instead the first candle lit on the Advent wreath, a reminder of Christ, the light shining in every darkness. Ask him for the clarity you need to assess your options and make good decisions that will bring you home to the heart of this holy season.

Prayer: Lord Jesus, Light of the World, be a lamp to our feet as we walk through the lengthening dark toward the light that shines from the manger on Christmas Day.

No Harm or Hurt on God's Mountain

Readings: Isa 11:1-10; Luke 10:21-24

Scripture:
"Blessed are the eyes that see what you see." (Luke 10:23)

Reflection: What did the disciples see? They saw Jesus without yet knowing he was the One who would make true Isaiah's famous prophecy of the mountain where lambs would host wolves, leopards and kid goats would nap together, calves and lions would share the grass, and there would be no harm to anyone. What Christmas goes by without a card that paints that holy scene before our longing eyes, as we listen to background news reports of children sucked into trafficking rings that destroy them, teenagers fed a diet of narcotics to the cartels' profit, schoolgirls kidnapped by extremist groups, and violence everywhere?

What Isaiah promises is not a radical personality change. On God's holy mountain, lions will still be recognizable as lions, sheep will grow no defenses, wolves will bare sharp teeth and sharper claws, bears will roar. What Isaiah promises is a radical change in relationships. Though leopards won't change their spots or snakes their slither, we will see no sign of predators and prey. The large and fierce will not eat the small and weak. The small and weak will not fear them.

How can that happen? We've tried better school security, tighter law enforcement, bigger and better weapons, multimillion-dollar rescue programs, and they have failed. What God tried was to send his own beloved Son into a world of predators and prey, evil devourers and human fodder to remake twisted humanity into the image of the God of love we were made to be. It seemed an act of folly. What could a vulnerable child do in a world of lions and wolves? He could relive the human story as a tale of mutual care rather than mutual destruction, of putting others before one's own whims and safeties, and, in the end, of surrendering his own life to the greatest predator of all, evil—and in so doing, defeating it. Evil feeds on and feeds human sinful selfishness. Christ offered himself as prey in our place.

Finding better methods to wipe out the predators is not the way. Living the life of Christ in such a way that everyone will see what the disciples saw—God's love made flesh in the crib and on the cross—is. When the whole world is filled with the experience of the new Messiah, we will all sit down at a new banquet and feed one another rather than feeding *on* one another.

Meditation: Who are the "predators" in your life? Would anyone think of you as a predator, nibbling away at self-esteem or gentleness or love? How can you change those relationships?

Prayer: Christ, our peace, let us see your face, let us learn your way, let us grow into your love that we may serve the birth of true peace in our immediate surroundings.

Everybody Come!

Readings: Isa 25:6-10a; Matt 15:29-37

Scripture:
On this mountain the LORD of hosts
will provide for all peoples
A feast of rich food and choice wines,
juicy, rich food and pure, choice wines.
On this mountain he will destroy . . . death forever.
The Lord GOD will wipe away
the tears from all faces. (Isa 25:6-7)

Reflection: God, ever the best of hosts, is sending out invitations to a great feast. What a menu! Rich foods, choice wines. A feast for royalty! But look at the guest list: "all peoples." *Everyone* is invited.

The gospel gives us a preview of the gathering on God's mountain in the story of the great picnic on a Galilean hillside, where Jesus provided more than plenty for all comers. They included folks not usually invited to banquets: "the lame, the blind, the deformed, the mute, and many others," and those who brought them. No one asked for IDs at the gate or sent the raggedly clad to sit in the back rows or drove the troublemakers off. First Jesus cured the sufferers of all those painful physical reminders of mortality. Then, ever a practical pastor, Jesus noticed that their stomachs were growling, so he and the disciples fed them with enough bread and fish for everyone to eat their fill—and lots of leftovers for them to pack up and take home. Ample food, death driven back, tears wiped away, as the prophet foretold. Quite a banquet!

In Advent, we look forward to the final banquet in the new Jerusalem and yet prepare to remember with joy the first arrival of the Christ Child in Bethlehem, which fittingly means "House of Bread." But today and every day we receive our own invitations to God's banquet of Word and Bread and Wine. There Christ, himself ample food, death's defeat, and grief's destroyer, will feed us our daily bread, lead us a little closer to eternal life, and wipe away our tears with his compassion.

Meditation: The daily invitation to the banquet of life sits on your heart's mantelpiece. Will you leave it there unopened because you're afraid you really don't measure up, you really don't have the right clothes, you're a little worn around the edges, you're . . . well, inadequate? Read Isaiah's promise again: everyone is invited! Read the story of the great picnic Jesus hosts: lame, deformed, mute, and lots of folks just like you are there. "Your presence is requested," says the invitation. And there's a P.S.: "Please come!"

Prayer: O God, Giver of all good gifts, open our hearts to trust your word, your promise, your desire to include us at the feast on the mountain, and your abiding love that calls, heals, and feeds us always.

How Firm a Foundation!

Readings: Isa 26:1-6; Matt 7:21, 24-27

Scripture:
"Everyone who listens to these words of mine and acts on
  them
will be like a wise man who built his house on rock.
The rain fell, the floods came,
and the winds blew and buffeted the house.
But it did not collapse; it had been set solidly on rock."
  (Matt 7:24-25)

Reflection: December weather is chancy at best—blizzards, ice storms, rains abounding. Hardly the season when a wise builder lays the foundation for a house!

Yet God did just that, at least according to the liturgical calendar. As the Advent readings remind us, God began the preparations for that foundation millennia ago, with count-less ordinary people just like us called to help carry out through many ups and downs God's plans to make ready the foundation for the world's future: the Rock who is Christ (see 1 Cor 10:1-5).

But what a frail foundation he first looked! When the crèche goes up, look at the figures: the ox and ass standing guard, Mary and Joseph praying, shepherds and magi on the way. Compare the infant Jesus, hidden till Christmas—he looks so tiny, so powerless, so vulnerable beside all these bigger figures. How can God possibly build a house, never mind a kingdom, on this fragile little foundation? And how can we entrust our lives to it in faith?

God didn't. And we don't. The house's foundation is God's enduring Word of love made flesh. That's the unfailing Rock hidden in the Child but made visible as time goes by. His strength was tested and built up over years: a risky childhood, a carpenter-builder's hardworking youth, and, finally, the storm. When he went public, the rains fell, floods of contradictions rose, and angry winds threatened to blow him away, this upstart teacher opposed by religious and political authorities alike as he went about unarmed and unshielded, changing hearts with words, lives with healing and forgiveness, the rich with challenges, and the poor with bread. In the end, abandoned, betrayed, denied, mocked, and tortured, he died among thieves.

Then the unimaginable! He rose from the dead! God's house, our home built on this unfailing Rock, stands forever.

Meditation: In the crèche, look at the two rocks of faith, Mary and Joseph, who raised the Child. Think about the storms that would weather them all. What or who is your faith founded on? What threatens it? What shelters and strengthens it—or rather *who* does?

Prayer: Christ our Rock, hold us fast in faith when the rains fall, the floods come, and the winds of life blow. Let us trust and hold on!

December 7:
Saint Ambrose, Bishop and Doctor of the Church

What Do You See?

Readings: Isa 29:17-24; Matt 9:27-31

Scripture:
Then [Jesus] touched their eyes and said,
"Let it be done for you according to your faith."
And their eyes were opened. (Matt 9:29-30)

Reflection: A religious sister who had suffered severely impaired vision for years finally had corrective surgery. At her first recreation with the community in a walled courtyard after her recovery, she seemed deaf to the conversation as she studied her surroundings. Suddenly, she exclaimed with delight, "I never knew there were *vines* on that wall!"

After Jesus had healed the two blind men what did they see that they had never seen before? Jesus, certainly. Did he look anything like the one they had imagined when they called out to him, "Son of David, have pity on us"? What about family members, friends, neighbors? How did they look?

Conversion begins with the gift of sight we call faith, but it's not always a comfortable gift. Today's saint, St. Ambrose, a devoted student of Scripture, baptized many a new convert to Catholicism, but none more famous than St. Augustine. Augustine's conversion began with the discovery that the truth he had long sought is apt to strip away illusions about the world as we had imagined it rather than as we, like the blind beggars, discover it to be. Augustine was a brilliant student of literature and a polished public speaker by profession. During his years of searching, he had come across the Bible and discarded it as rough and primitive. Then, one day, hearing a voice saying, "Take and read," he picked up St. Paul's letter to the Romans and read a powerful passage that suddenly convinced him to abandon his sinful lifestyle and take on life in the Christ he had never really seen. Becoming committed to the Bible, he counted himself another blind man to whom Jesus had given sight.

The Advent readings offer us daily opportunities to see Christ, the world, and ourselves anew through the multifaceted lenses of the Scriptures. Sometimes they reinforce cherished convictions. Sometimes they strip away cherished illusions. Always they invite us to look with new eyes and discover more deeply who Christ is for us and our world, and who we are for Christ and our world. Exciting? Sometimes. Reassuring? Sometimes. Demanding? Always. Take and read!

Meditation: Who has opened your eyes to the Christ of the Scriptures? How? For whom have you opened, or are you called to open, the eyes of others? How does your life convince others to "take and read"?

Prayer: O Christ, living Word of God, open our eyes to see you more clearly, love you more dearly, and follow you more nearly.

December 8: Immaculate Conception of the
Blessed Virgin Mary

About-Face!

Readings: Gen 3:9-15, 20; Eph 1:3-6, 11-12; Luke 1:26-38

Scripture:
Blessed be the God and Father of our Lord Jesus Christ,
. . . as he chose us in him, before the foundation of the
   world,
to be holy and without blemish before him. (Eph 1:3-4)

Reflection: God's original plan went awry when the serpent in the garden turned Eve's head. As she walked through this bright new world filled with wonders, a voice she had not heard before captured her attention. Already dangerously expert in humanity, the serpent drew her eyes to another enchantment: a luscious piece of fruit. With some clever conversational sleight of tongue, the serpent persuaded her to look away from God's bigger picture and focus on her own undiscovered and unexplored desires. The fruit looked good. The tree looked pretty. It looked like it would give her wisdom (definitely inexperience talking!). So she forgot about God, took a bite, and shared it with Adam. We read the consequences in today's first reading.

Unlike Eve's face after that tricky bit of twisting, Mary's face was turned away from her own interests and toward God's and her neighbors' from the start. No doubt the

Tempter was thwarted by this second blameless visage after Adam and Eve's had been besmirched. Perhaps he tried again with Mary, hunting for some new fruit that would get this new sinless one's attention off God and onto herself. We don't know that part of her story, but we do know she never listened. The Voice and the Word that filled her life were God's. Self, that flag the Tempter waved so successfully before Eve's eyes, held no appeal. Her life of "yes" left no place for "no," except when the Tempter was asking.

God has never rescinded the original plan. In Mary, God turned the human face back in the right direction. The gift was divine—we call it immaculate conception—but all through Mary's life, the choice was hers. Whichever direction the human being is facing, the freedom and responsibility to choose or refuse love remain.

We ourselves enter the scene contorted by a long history of human refusal, but we are nevertheless baptized into the graced capacity to say yes to God's plan and no to the Tempter's.

Meditation: When you find yourself focused solely on your own interests, what keeps you from "turning around"—another word for conversion. Ask Mary's help—she has been working at turning God's children's heads toward love for a very long time.

Prayer: O Mary, conceived without sin, pray for me that I may turn away from myself and toward Christ.

SECOND WEEK OF ADVENT

Homecoming

Readings: Bar 5:1-9; Phil 1:4-6, 8-11; Luke 3:1-6

Scripture:
Up, Jerusalem! stand upon the heights;
look to the east and see your children
gathered from the east and the west. . . .
Led away on foot by their enemies they left you:
but God will bring them back to you
borne aloft in glory as on royal thrones. (Bar 5:5-6)

Reflection: In the gospel, John the Baptist takes up Isaiah's Advent exhortation: "Prepare the way of the Lord." Still quoting, John urges us to clear away all the stumbling blocks that might make God's road difficult. Why? Can't God handle a few curves in the road, or a mountain or two?

Actually, the landscaping seems to be not for God's sake but for the sake of the Redeemer's retinue. And what an unlikely retinue it is! John promises we'll see "the salvation of God." Baruch puts human faces on "the salvation": God is bringing back home to Jerusalem those deported and scattered long before by harsh conquerors in a bloody invasion of God's city. Many of those who survived would have been elderly by the time of their return. Their progeny came as strangers to a city they had never seen. Modern photos and videos fill in images of scarred, emaciated, fragile men, women, and children in other lands liberated from conquest and captivity, many hardly able to walk. Rough roads would undo them. With touching compassion, Baruch seats them on royal thrones borne aloft on others' shoulders. They are "God's salvation" in the flesh, welcomed with honor.

What Baruch couldn't know is that the One who would bring them was himself born into a human race exiled from Eden and ruled ever since by the conquering powers of sin and death. He came as a slave among slaves (see Phil 2:7), visiting human beings of every era in all the places of our enslavement to sin, sickness, and death in order to carry us out with him. And we don't make that pretty a picture either, scarred as we are by our own wrongdoing and others', stumbling as we do in Christ's new light after a long darkness that we had ceased to recognize as the shadow of death.

It doesn't matter. Whoever we are, however we are, wherever we come from, we are "God's salvation," and we are welcome home.

Meditation: The familiar "I'll Be Home for Christmas" is a promise soaked in nostalgia and wishful thinking. God's promise of homecoming, realized by Christ's advents in past, present, and future, is the reality. It's not usually accompanied by prophetic fanfares and royal thrones. It's offered in the quiet of our hearts by prayer, word, sacrament, and community. Come on, let's go!

Prayer: O Christ, you promised to prepare a place for us and return to take us there. Make our hearts and our lives ready to go with you.

The High Road

Readings: Isa 35:1-10; Luke 5:17-26

Scripture:
A highway will be there,
called the holy way;
No one unclean may pass over it. . . .
[A]nd on it the redeemed will walk.
Those whom the LORD has ransomed will return
and enter Zion singing,
crowned with everlasting joy. (Isa 35:8, 10)

Reflection: Just imagine! A highway better than the yellow brick road! Dorothy and crew, or anyone else, can travel it safely because it's too high for the lions and tigers and bears growling below to reach. Look! All those exiled from Jerusalem by alien conquerors, all walking or skipping or dancing along the road, singing as they go! And we are invited to join them.

But what if we're one of the unclean—those banished from the highway for diseases of body or soul? What if we're one of the paralyzed who can't even walk, never mind skip or dance? Are we unwelcome, condemned to stand on the sidelines, watching the joyful crowd go by without us? Is there a sign: "Holy Way—sinners keep off!"?

Jesus says a categorical "No!" True, only the redeemed can walk this road, so Jesus stations himself at the on-ramp, on the lookout for those whose approach would set off alarms, swing barriers in place, and trigger the disapproving voice we fear to hear, "You are not allowed here!"

Jesus removes whatever bars the way to the unwanted and the unworthy. In today's gospel, he heals a sufferer paralyzed, so the story implies, by his sins, like all those whose spirit has been frozen into inertia by sinful habits and destructive behaviors. Jesus has a cure: forgiveness. It's not cheap. It comes at the price of faith and the willingness to change. The forgiven must get up and walk away from the immobilizing past of wrong thinking and wrongdoing. Sometimes, they may need a little help from their friends to get to that point—like the paralytic's friends with their creative determination to get the man to Jesus. Forgiven and healed by Jesus' love, this paralytic and all the unclean and the unable can walk right up that on-ramp onto the highway, carrying passes stamped, "Redeemed!"

Meditation: Do you feel excluded from the highway the saints have traveled because you're just an unworthy sinner? Or do you frown on others you think unworthy to walk there? Or are you one of the scouts Jesus seems to send out to find the unclean and the unwanted and bring them in? Think of times when you may have played any or all of these parts.

Prayer: Jesus, Great Healer, let us all walk home joyfully on the highway of the redeemed, helping one another as we go.

The Shepherd

Readings: Isa 40:1-11; Matt 18:12-14

Scripture:
"If a man has a hundred sheep and one of them goes astray,
will he not leave the ninety-nine in the hills
and go in search of the stray?" (Matt 18:12)

Reflection: A man with a hundred sheep is doing pretty well financially, so why would he risk ninety-nine to go looking for a single stray? Strange economics! Our monastery is surrounded by vast cattle ranches where the cattle roam unsupervised. Come roundup time, a few are usually missing, but the ranchers just cut their losses, reckoning that three or four or ten head aren't worth the time, trouble, and money it would cost to find them.

The Good Shepherd's economics are vastly different from ours. He isn't counting sums; he's counting people. Is that stubborn ewe plotting a way into the neighbor's field—again? And that young ram, lowering his horns and charging at shadows—will he grow up to be as stubborn and uncooperative as he is right now? And those two! What are they fighting over now? No matter. There are no perfect sheep in this flock, and the Shepherd knows it. But there are no unwanted sheep either.

One is gone? The Shepherd knows which one. He knows them all by name, all one hundred. He looks around at them.

The bellwether will keep the rest together till he gets back. And the old ram will protect them should wolves come prowling. But the missing one—a sheep alone—is a sheep in danger. He has to go after it.

He knows the risks. A sheep in pursuit of greener grass and glorious freedom can travel a long way in a short time, unaware of danger. The Shepherd knows what it is to hazard the steep climb down the cliff to the sheep shivering on a narrow ledge below. And his hands are scarred from wrestling a youngling out of a thornbush. But he will do anything to keep from losing even one. Anything.

It's not a matter of financial profit and loss for this Shepherd. His investment isn't cash. It's love.

Meditation: As long as we pay more attention to our gain than to another's good, Jesus' refusal to watch his own back, to count the cost before he takes the risk, to write off bad investments—such as Peter on Holy Thursday night, for example—will never make any sense to us. But his cross haunts us when we wonder if our own flock of responsibilities is worth the trouble—or if we are. Lost or found or simply perplexed, the Advent promise remains our strength: Christ our Shepherd is coming!

Prayer: Christ, Good Shepherd, stay with us, guard us, guide us always! Bring us safely home!

December 12:
Our Lady of Guadalupe

Mother to Us All

Readings: Zech 2:14-17 or Rev 11:19a; 12:1-6a, 10ab; Luke 1:26-38 or Luke 1:39-47

Scripture:
"And how does this happen to me,
that the mother of my Lord should come to me?" (Luke 1:43)

Reflection: We think of Mary in Nazareth, the Judean hill country, Bethlehem, heaven. Mary's geography often seems to put her at a distance in time, space, holiness. Artists have emphasized her remoteness by robing her in styles we'll never see in the supermarket and giving her a beauty of face and a serenity that don't walk through our parking lots. Our Lady of Guadalupe seems to fit that pattern. A young, pregnant, peaceful woman, Aztec in appearance and speech, clad in robes hinting at royalty and Aztec religious beliefs, adorned with the sun, moon, and stars (see Rev 12:1), she is far too exotic to live on our block. She was born in first-century Palestine, appeared to Juan Diego in sixteenth-century Mexico City, and does not breathe our town's polluted air.

But we, her Son's sisters and brothers, indeed his Body, know that these distance markers are irrelevant. Wherever we are, whenever we are, we have always recognized her as one of us, like us but beyond us in holiness and faith, yet always seeking us out and urging us to come along with her. She remembers, you see. She remembers wrapping her Child in swaddling clothes, nursing him, playing with him, cleaning him up. We can imagine her remembering when she demanded he eat his vegetables, bandaged his thumb after the hammer went astray—and worried about him as he set off on the journey from which he never really came home. We have seen great works of art depicting her holding his lifeless body in her lap. How could she, the mother, not continue to care for the Body of the One whose body she bore, cared for, and buried?

So wherever we celebrate this feast, in Mexico or Rio de Janeiro or Ontario or our neighborhood in Anytown, USA, we honor her as patroness of the Americas and as the mother who will never abandon us in our many appalling needs. We know from experience that all the apparent distance of time and place and culture is merely a shadow across the real truth of her abiding presence and love.

Meditation: Sit before an image of Our Lady of Guadalupe. Look past her differences of face and dress to the unchanging truth of her universal motherhood. Talk to her about what concerns you, trusting she will understand and care.

Prayer: Our Lady of Guadalupe, mother of the world, pray for us!

December 13:
Saint Lucy, Virgin and Martyr

Thirsty?

Readings: Isa 41:13-20; Matt 11:11-15

Scripture:
The afflicted and the needy seek water in vain,
their tongues are parched with thirst.
I, the LORD, will answer them . . . . (Isa 41:17)

Reflection: Thirst is mortality's tap on our shoulder, reminding us that for all our cultures' achievements, we are still utterly dependent on something we take for granted in most of North America: water. The doctor warns us: "Drink more water! That will take care of your headache, fatigue, itching skin . . ." You know the rest of the list. Water shortages, water pollution, water systems' vulnerability to attack are all topics of urgent concern throughout the world. We can survive a remarkably long time without food, but not without water.

Isaiah's people were all too familiar with the threat posed by its lack. Drought was a seasonal threat. Access to wells was sometimes held hostage by the powerful for the sake of squeezing profits from the poor, as this passage suggests. Enemies blocked off water supplies to besieged cities. Water was and is a necessity no one can afford to lose.

But there is a deeper necessity, one easily denied or ignored in our increasingly secularized world: the thirst for God.

When the human spirit seeks some transcendence and finds only dry streambeds in established religions, we often spin mirages out of our need and try to slake our thirst from wells that are not there. Science, entertainment, invented deities, and many other sources seem to offer refreshment for our thirst but in the end turn out to be dry cisterns.

In the gospel acclamation, Isaiah offers a prayer on behalf of those desperate in their thirst: "Let the clouds rain down the Just One, / and the earth bring forth a Savior" (Isa 45:8, translated from the Vulgate). The Just One who will truly quench our deepest thirst is the One whose birth we prepare to celebrate, whose final coming we await with joyful hope, and whose daily advent we welcome gratefully in all the ways the Savior comes to us through life on "the earth."

Meditation: Next time you're thirsty, consider what deep thirsts of the spirit tap on your shoulder and how Christ responds to them with living water. Consider trying a little more prayer time, reading the Bible more regularly, spending a few minutes in the evening looking back over the day to see where and how Christ came into it.

Prayer: O God, Giver of all good gifts, let even the clouds that sometimes darken our life rain down the Just One and fill our parched moments with living water!

New Song, New Dance

Readings: Isa 48:17-19; Matt 11:16-19

Scripture:
"To what shall I compare this generation?
It is like children who sit in marketplaces and call to one
   another,
'We played the flute for you, but you did not dance,
we sang a dirge but you did not mourn.'" (Matt 11:16)

Reflection: Isn't this just like us at our most childish? We called the tune, and Christ wouldn't dance to it, so now we're peeved. If we're like Jesus' audience (and we are), we're not even sure which dance we really wanted. John the Baptist came fasting, and they didn't like that. Jesus came eating and drinking, and they didn't like that. But perhaps the tune is not the problem. Perhaps what we human beings really want is the right to call the tune, whatever it is.

Our history should warn us. God created a magnificent universe where all things worked together in harmony. Persuaded by the Tempter, who is apparently not fond of harmony of any kind, the first couple chose a tune of their own—and set off a dreadful cacophony as all the instruments in the primal orchestra ceased to listen to one another. And, having shut their ears to God's voice, human beings became tone deaf.

God expresses exasperation in today's first reading: "I . . . teach you what is for your good. . . . / If you would hearken to my commandments / your prosperity would be like a river . . ." (Isa 48:17-18). Jesus echoes it in the gospel.

Listen! God's insistence echoes down through the ages in the Scriptures. Saint Benedict proposes a new approach: your ordinary ears may be deaf to God's voice, so listen with the ears of your heart instead! The fruit is obedience: instead of trying to call the dance tune for God, we allow God to call the tune for us. We are not bad dance partners when we do—look at all the saints!

Of course, our listening may put us out of step with the world around us. Henry David Thoreau (1817–62) had a famous answer for that: "If a man does not keep pace with his companions, perhaps it is because he hears a different drummer. Let him step to the music which he hears, however measured or far away." Jesus did. And he is the best dance partner of all, regardless of the discontent of those children in the marketplace.

Meditation: If the conflicting voices of this season leave you feeling torn and confused about your next step, go deep into your own heart and listen there for the voice of God, which sings our inner chaos into harmony.

Prayer: O Christ, God's living love song to a world in turmoil, open our hearts' ears to hear you and follow your lead in the daily dance.

The Advent Balance

Readings: Sir 48:1-4, 9-11; Matt 17:9a, 10-13

Scripture:
[L]ike a fire there appeared the prophet Elijah
whose words were as a flaming furnace.
By the Lord's word he shut up the heavens
and three times brought down fire. (Sir 48:1, 3)

Reflection: At the time of Jesus' discussion with the disciples about Elijah's expected return as harbinger of the Messiah, John the Baptist is already dead, but his memory clearly burns in Jesus' mind. John's was indeed a fiery voice. He stood firmly in the line of the great classical prophets like Isaiah and Jeremiah, but he lacked the tenderness they sometimes displayed. John sounded angry, and he seemed to promise an angry messiah, a judge with all the fearsome fire of Elijah himself. John came demanding repentance even of scribes and Pharisees with very dire threats against those who refused: an axe at the roots of fruitless trees, fire to consume the dead wood like chaff.

Jesus carried no axe. He did say, "I have come to set the earth on fire, and how I wish it were already blazing!" (Luke 12:49), but what he yearned for was the transforming Spirit, who appears in fire at Pentecost, as God appeared in a fiery cloud in the Old Testament. Here, fire is the language not of anger but of divine love so intense it burns away all inessentials and sets the redeemed free to live, perhaps for the first time.

While John was alive but in prison, he had sent messengers to ask Jesus if he was the promised one to come, and Jesus sent them back with a list of his credentials: the blind see, the lame walk, lepers are healed, the deaf hear, and the poor have been fed on the good news of God's reign. Here are the signs of the burning Spirit of God at work! Not what John imagined but what God did.

Advent promises not fire and brimstone but the work of sin and death transformed into profound and lasting life by the power of the creative Spirit working through the Christ, God's love for us made human flesh. This is not John's threat. It is Jesus' promise.

Meditation: John is an uncomfortable prophet. We might prefer Isaiah's more consoling prophecies of sheep carried home by a gentle Shepherd. We read those too, but John will not let us soft-pedal the radical transformation Christ's coming brings to lives captive to sin. Christ, the Truth, will set us free—but freedom can be very uncomfortable indeed to those accustomed to their prison. What does your prison look like? Are you at home there? Why? Are you willing to leave? Why not?

Prayer: O Spirit of God, fire of life, burn away in us all that keeps us from receiving Christ and living fully in him!

THIRD WEEK OF ADVENT

Good News!

Readings: Zeph 3:14-18a; Phil 4:4-7; Luke 3:10-18

Scripture:
Exhorting them in many other ways,
[John] preached good news to the people. (Luke 3:18)

Reflection: It doesn't sound like good news. John had just told the candidates for baptism, including even tax collectors and soldiers, that they must straighten up and fly right: share all extra clothes and food with those who have none, give up your profiteering and false accusations—oh, and quit grumbling about your salary. I doubt these words brought joy to anyone's heart, especially when John backed them up with the promise (or was it a threat?) of a coming messiah who would baptize them with fire, winnow out the wheat from the chaff, and burn the chaff "with unquenchable fire." They all knew it was not farm crops he was talking about.

The odd thing is that for all his harsh directness, John really was preaching good news. His hearers came to him for a baptism of repentance—large crowds of them, even scribes and Pharisees along with tax collectors and soldiers—because they wanted to change. They knew, obviously, that there were things they needed to repent of and wanted to put behind them, even if it meant throwing their bad behavior in the fire to be burned to ash so that it could not return.

It would be only much later they would learn that the transforming fire brought by the Messiah was not the fire of Gehenna but the unquenchable fire of the Holy Spirit, God's love at work as we saw yesterday.

The first reading tells us that the news was good not only for those to be redeemed and made new, as they wanted to be, but even more so for God. Today is known as Gaudete Sunday, from the first word of the entrance song in Latin, "Rejoice!" It's borrowed from St. Paul's letter to the Philippians, today's second reading, which exhorts us, "Rejoice in the Lord always." But Zephaniah reports in the first reading that God, having removed all those things John urges people to drop, and more besides, will join in the rejoicing too: "The Lord, your God . . . will rejoice over you with gladness, / and renew you in his love, / he will sing joyfully because of you, / as one sings at festivals." We hear perhaps too often that we should not grieve God by our sins, but here the prophet reports very good news indeed: we will set God to singing with joy when we allow the Redeemer to take our sins away.

Meditation: God loves us very much and wants the best for us. What habits of thought, word, and deed do you think God would really like to free you from?

Prayer: God of love, transform in us what most keeps us, and those who love us, from singing songs of rejoicing with you this Christmas!

Wisdom's Family Tree

Readings: Gen 49:2, 8-10; Matt 1:1-17

Scripture:
O Wisdom of our God Most High,
guiding creation with power and love:
come to teach us the path of knowledge! (gospel acclamation, cf. Isa 11:2-3; Wis 8:1)

Reflection: The days of late Advent we sing the "O Antiphons," a series of seven ancient meditative refrains that address the awaited Messiah with Old Testament images connecting the expected One to God. Borrowed from the Liturgy of the Hours, they now appear as gospel acclamations on December 17–23.

Today, the first O Antiphon, praising Wisdom, introduces Jesus' genealogy. The choice is appropriate: St. Paul attaches the rich Old Testament image of Wisdom to Christ, "the wisdom of God" (1 Cor 1:24).

All of us are heirs to the long accumulation of wisdom that runs like sap through our family tree, strengthening us to live wisely ourselves so that we can pass our own wisdom on to future generations. Jesus' family history is a meditation on the wisdom tradition into which the Word of God was born in the flesh.

Jesus' ancestors are rooted in the larger history of God's people and so are defined by their relationship with God:

some were faithful, some strayed, some sinned but repented, some wandered in from other traditions and were adopted as members of the family. Commentaries tend to focus on the honored elders like the faithful patriarch Abraham, the sinners like the courageous prostitute Rahab, and even the foreigners like Ruth. All of them struggled, learned, chose, and then handed their wisdom on.

But while some of Jesus' ancestors were famous and some infamous, most, it seems, were so ordinary that they are remembered only as names. All we know about them is that they too made their contribution by struggling, learning, choosing well or ill, and handling their anonymous wisdom down through the tree whose greatest fruit was Jesus.

Spiritually, we are the fruit of the same tree, "joint heirs with Christ," says St. Paul in a different context (Rom 8:16-17), as are all those baptized into his Body since. Like our predecessors, we must struggle, learn, choose well or ill, and then hand on our own wisdom to the next generation of God's people even if we, like so many of Jesus' ancestors, remain only names in the genealogy.

Meditation: In Jesus' genealogy, we hear the roll call of those who went before us and stand behind us, urging us too to hand the wisdom on. Whose names would you add to the roll? Why?

Prayer: O Christ, Wisdom of God, teach us the wisdom of the gospel, and strengthen us to hand it on any way we can.

Beside a Pool of Quiet

Readings: Jer 23:5-8; Matt 1:18-25

Scripture:
Joseph . . . was a righteous man. (Matt 1:19)

Reflection: If you are fortunate, you know someone who is "a pool of quiet." If you are doubly fortunate, you are one yourself.

St. Joseph was.

Not because he didn't talk, as we sometimes think. He says nothing in the gospel accounts, but his interlocutor was an angel who spoke to him in dreams where no answer was required. If he hadn't talked under normal circumstances, the villagers would not later have remembered him as too ordinary to be family to the Messiah.

Not because he had no worries or because his life was uneventful either. The discovery of Mary's pregnancy, the dream of an angel revealing the startling news of the child's father, the order to report to Bethlehem even before the baby's birth, the lack of any accommodations but a stable, the urgent order to head out for Egypt because of Herod's rage, the business of finding home and work in a foreign country, the order to return home when the coast was clear—these are not the hallmarks of a trouble-free life!

Joseph's quiet didn't come from outside circumstances. It came, as quiet always does, from the inside. Joseph was simply himself, fully himself, and nothing else. Faithfulness to one's own truth is often called integrity. Righteousness and integrity go hand in hand. Righteousness is moral goodness or obedience to moral laws; integrity is honesty and fairness. They reflect a person who is inwardly whole, whatever life's circumstances. And Joseph was.

Though the gospels do not say so, we must assume that Joseph's wholeness came under attack from the Tempter, who has a sharp nose for what God has made whole, and who quickly tries to tear it apart. Integrity is anathema in evil's realm, as we see in Eden and in Jesus' temptations in the desert. We can imagine what the Tempter whispered: "Marry her? She's an adulteress. Only a simpleton believes in dreams!" Or: "Take off for Egypt? Surely you don't think the king has any interest in a carpenter's family!"

Joseph made no answer except action. What God told him through the angel, he believed and did, let the chips fall where they may. Thus Joseph lived in inner quiet in the midst of outward chaos. So can we.

Meditation: Do you know someone in whose company others find peace? What makes it so? How can you be that person in this busy season?

Prayer: Quiet St. Joseph, teach us to listen to Christ, our peace, and to do as he tells us so that we too may become a quiet source of peace.

Bad News, Good News

Readings: Judg 13:2-7, 24-25a; Luke 1:5-25

Scripture:
He who is to come will come and will not delay,
and now there will be no fear within our land,
for he is our Savior. (entrance antiphon, cf. Heb 10:37)

Reflection: In the stories surrounding Jesus' birth, the angel Gabriel is given the thankless task of bringing the Good News to people who find the angel frightening and the news discomforting. Today we read the story of Gabriel's announcement to Zechariah that he and his wife Elizabeth will have a son, though they are old and so far childless. The son will be John the Baptist.

The entrance antiphon makes a very firm promise appropriate six days before Christmas: look for the Savior soon. That's followed by another very firm promise that isn't quite so certain: "now there will be no fear within our land." Why no fear? Because "he is our Savior."

This is an instance of good news shoveling the bad news under the rug, a practice quite common in ritual celebrations like Christmas. But what is the bad news that makes Zechariah, and later the Virgin Mary, and still later us, quake a bit around the knees?

For Zechariah, who doubts, and Mary, who believes, it might be the responsibility of bearing and raising a child who will bring God's deliverance to a world entangled in sin and death. "Who am I," both of them could say, "to usher the Messiah into this world?"

For us, though, it might be the very announcement itself: a redeemer is coming. Redemption is scary news wrapped up in glad tidings because it means something is going to change, and change radically. The cautious banker hidden within all of us is already toting up the cost: What will I have to give up?

No one much likes change. All of us have some selfish thoughts and desires we try to keep hidden away. And we know perfectly well, because we've heard the gospel before, that they'll have to go, along with our favorite sins, the bits of conversion we've been putting off, our couch potato approach to growth in holiness. Redemption costs.

Today is a good time to be honest about our resistances to salvation but an even better time to recognize what Zechariah and Mary knew: whatever the cost, redemption is the pearl of great price, worth selling everything else for. The bad news is very short lived, like the pain of having a tooth pulled. The Good News banishes fear forever!

Meditation: What are you most afraid of losing if you buy fully into God's plan of salvation? Why?

Prayer: Great Gift of God, Jesus Christ our Savior, quiet our selfish fears with the joy of your coming that we may welcome you with open hearts on Christmas.

Expectant

Readings: Isa 7:10-14; Luke 1:26-38

Scripture:
The virgin shall conceive and bear a son. (Isa 7:14)

Reflection: In Mary's world, childbearing fulfilled God's first command to humanity: "Be fertile and multiply." (Gen 1:28). By contrast, childlessness was held in some disgrace. It seemed a failure in obedience to the Creator, even when a couple was not childless by choice as in the case of the Baptist's parents. In that cultural context, virginity was valued as preparation for childbirth within the chosen family setting. Although we sometimes hear that all the women of Israel hoped to be chosen to bear the Messiah, that seems unlikely. Expectations of the Messiah varied widely both in urgency and in content from place to place and time to time. Messianic hope may have formed a vague backdrop to the desire for children but that desire was primarily an expression of obedience to God's plan for creation.

Mary was a young woman of her time and place but one conditioned by a unique personal relationship to God in her sinlessness. Since her love for God (and neighbor) was unhindered by any trace of self-interest, all her desire would have been for the good God wanted to achieve for this beloved world. She had no way of knowing what that would mean, but whatever it meant, she was willing and ready.

Mary, in her virginity, is an icon of empty expectation waiting eagerly to be filled. She is the mother and mirror of the Advent world still waiting in darkness in so many places for the coming of God's Promised One. Mary's expectation is different than ours: she simply waited for the child God would send her if that was God's plan for her. We are more inclined to fill the emptiness of waiting with daydreams of what such fulfillment will look like: what we will find under the Christmas tree, what the political organization of a world at peace should be, what humanity's "salvation" will look like according to the perfect picture of human potential we have painted and now work for.

Mary knew better than we do that expectation with its face toward God can't be bothered with such pictures and plans—because God's gift is always a surprise. Look at how Mary's empty expectancy was filled!

Meditation: How do you experience emptiness and expectation as you look forward to Christmas? How do you hope for God to fill it—friends, family, peace among quarrelers, or material pleasures to dull your painful longings? How can you cultivate a hope emptied of self and ready to receive God's gifts?

Prayer: Mary, icon of Advent, pray for us, that we may make the inner room to receive God's true gifts at Christmas.

Here He Comes!

Readings: Song 2:8-14 or Zeph 3:14-18a; Luke 1:39-45

Scripture:
[H]ere he comes. . . .
Here he stands behind our wall,
gazing through the windows,
peering through the lattices. (Song 2:8, 9b)

Reflection: Christmas is almost here! In fact, Christ is actually here now, as he always is. Impatient to be with us—hard though we may find that to believe—he sometimes jumps the gun a little and raps on the window of our attention before December 25.

He is here, but sometimes we are not. We're busy studying our to-do list, worrying about finding the popular item a loved one wants, checking the pantry to see if we have enough for surprise guests. Or we've locked the door against the crowd of memories of Christmases past when family and friends were still around, because we dread the loneliness and depression that may follow them in. Or the demands of the job at holiday peak leave us too exhausted to bother with anyone or anything else. You can fill in your own scenario: What are you doing behind stout walls and shuttered windows?

Elderly Elizabeth, six months pregnant, probably coping with swollen feet and a backache, could quite understandably have stayed in seclusion when her young cousin dropped in with her unborn child. She could have sent the maid out to the front room with refreshments and apologies and an offer to put Mary up with a neighbor. Maybe they could visit for an hour tomorrow morning, if Elizabeth felt up to it? Company really was inconvenient right now. Surely Mary understood?

Think what Elizabeth would have missed! Think what we might miss when we shut ourselves up behind our busyness or loneliness or job demands! Open the door and let Jesus in, for heaven's sake—or rather for your own.

Meditation: Remember that Jesus may come hidden as he came to Elizabeth, hidden in his mother's womb. He might be concealed in a Christmas card from an estranged friend, or a phone call begging you to help out with parish food baskets, or in a child dying to tell you about the new puppy next door. He might break in on your loneliness as an aged acquaintance badly in need of sharing memories you're avoiding. He might preempt your boss in a sudden urge to pray a little.

Go ahead! Open up!

Prayer: St. Elizabeth, obtain for us the grace to recognize Christ in his every coming, however inconvenient, welcome him in, and spend some time with him who so wants to spend time with us.

December 22: Saturday of the Third Week of Advent

Rejoice in the Lord Always!

Readings: 1 Sam 1:24-28; Luke 1:46-56

Scripture:
"My soul proclaims the greatness of the Lord;
my spirit rejoices in God my savior.
for he has looked upon his lowly servant." (Luke 1:46-48)

Reflection: Are you a little grouchy as Christmas preparations take over your life? Are you a little teary-eyed about those who won't be there to celebrate with you? Are you a little guilty at the sight of people picking through the garbage bin behind the grocery store?

Time to look at what Mary is singing. Think about it. She's a young girl newly arrived at Elizabeth's after a ninety-mile journey on foot or donkey. She has a betrothed husband, but she is carrying a child not his. She can't give any explanation most people would understand. What does she have to praise God for?

She praises God first for his love for her. When the December skies are dark, the nights cold, the calendar stuffed fuller than any turkey, do you recognize God's personal and enduring love for you? Look around for a minute: See any signs of that love you might not have recognized amid your complaints? A card from a loved one, an excited kid with a face smeared with chocolate, a young person who offers to carry your groceries up the stairs for you, a homeless beggar who gives you a big smile for that quarter you dropped into the hat? (Christ has been known to lurk around in the form of a beggar.)

But Mary goes on almost immediately to praise God for the good he will do for others through her Son. It's good done the hard way. Tables will turn, maybe even on us, but the purpose of the turning is not punishment or revenge but restoring to even the hardest of hearts the capacity to love and live in the reign of God. Mary's son will go to unimaginable lengths to gather up everyone, rich or poor, well fed or starving, powerful or oppressed. That includes you and me, whatever mood we're in right now. The Messiah is an equal opportunity savior in the most literal sense.

Meditation: Ask Mary to help you turn whatever makes you grouchy, sorrowful, guilty, or annoyed into reasons for rejoicing. Translate your to-do list into gratitude for having purpose and ability; your grief for the absent into gladness for the presence they were; and your guilt into a stint at the parish packing baskets for the homeless. But if you're happy: pray Mary's song for those who aren't—yet.

Prayer: Mary, Mother of the Savior, teach us to find reasons for gratitude where there seem to be none and to rejoice always with you.

FOURTH WEEK OF ADVENT

Impossible Faith in an Inexplicable God

Readings: Mic 5:1-4a; Heb 10:5-10; Luke 1:39-45

Scripture:
"Blessed are you who believed
that what was spoken to you by the Lord
would be fulfilled." (Luke 1:45)

Reflection: In today's story, two mothers meet who shouldn't be mothers. One is too old, the other a virgin. They are cousins, but their deeper bond is the two things they have in common: an impossible pregnancy, and faith in an inexplicable God.

Do they think of Sarah, I wonder? She laughed when she overheard a strange visitor tell her husband she'd have a son, though she was too old. Do Mary and Elizabeth laugh together about their impossible children? They might. They are both, after all, filled with the Holy Spirit, whose fruit is joy.

Do they remember Sarah and Abraham's son? An impossible child promised and then born to an aging couple, an only son demanded back in sacrifice by an inexplicable God? This was no laughing matter. But courage is also the Spirit's gift.

Do Mary and Elizabeth wonder about their own impossible sons, promised and given by that same inexplicable God? Would God reclaim them again? Would God relent again as the knife was raised?

The two mothers didn't know, but we do. Yes, God would reclaim these only sons. No, this time God would not withhold the blade. Elizabeth probably didn't live to see her son die, but Mary did. She stood beneath the cross, an unwavering pillar of impossible faith in an inexplicable God even as her son drew his last breath.

Christmas is almost here. Tomorrow we will remember the birth of John the Baptist, Elizabeth's son. The next day we will celebrate the birth of Mary's son and share in her rejoicing. There is reason always for gladness in this impossible gift from a God whose love lies far beyond our understanding.

Meditation: Today, as we remember these two mothers who shouldn't be mothers, their two impossible children, and above all, their faith in their inexplicable God—who is also ours—let us ask them to share that faith with us. World catastrophes, family trials, and personal suffering don't stand back for Christmas. When winter darkness falls across the crib and our lives, as it must, let us also pray for their courage. The courage sustains the joy until the morning sun breaks through the night, as it did for Mary, and as it will for us.

Prayer: Holy Mothers Mary and Elizabeth, obtain for us the gift of faith that sustains Christmas joy even when circumstances challenge it, and the gift of courage to face the challenge.

I Promise!

Readings: 2 Sam 7:1-5, 8b-12, 14a, 16; Luke 1:67-79

Scripture:
"I will raise up your heir after you . . .
and I will make his Kingdom firm.
I will be a father to him,
and he shall be a son to me.
Your house and your Kingdom shall endure forever before
    me;
your throne shall stand firm forever." (2 Sam 7:12, 14a)

Reflection: God made this promise to King David near the end of his reign when all was peace and prosperity. It still burns as light no darkness can extinguish at a time when peace has become an elusive will-o'-the-wisp and prosperity is reserved for the few amid the millions who are starving. News headlines take turns warning of approaching disasters and offering reassurances that don't reassure. Kingdoms— political, financial, and fictional—rise and fall.

Against this dark night, God promises a firm kingdom, an enduring house, an immovable throne. Today's gospel offers the only lasting reassurance: "the dawn from on high shall break upon us, / to shine on those who dwell in darkness and the shadow of death, / and to guide our feet into the way of peace." The firm kingdom won't have a geographical capital, the enduring house is not made of stone mined from a local quarry, and the immovable throne won't ever appear in a TV show about the rich and famous. The firm kingdom stands on the power of God's word. The enduring house is not a building but a person, Jesus Christ, the new and eternal Temple not built by human hands. And the immovable throne is a wooden cross whose shadow is light that reaches into every corner of our darkness.

God is the great Promise Keeper. Tonight and tomorrow we will celebrate once again the promise fulfilled in the unlikely venue of a stable where a village girl and a carpenter treasure the newborn Child honored by strangers. Unnoticed then, still often unnoticed now, God's firm kingdom came long ago, and still stands. It brooks no conqueror, not even the invisible forces of sin and death.

So, even when this world's darkness grows and gathers, let us keep the night watch and rejoice again in the ancient words that still ring true: Glory to God in the highest! Peace, peace on earth! Tonight a savior is born!

Meditation: As you read and pray, look honestly at whatever darknesses threatens; then ask for the light to see through them and beyond them to God's enduring future, and place your trust in God's promise.

Prayer: Jesus Christ, the promised light and peace, come to us again in the approaching night, and shine within and among us for all time!

SEASON OF CHRISTMAS

How Many Syllables Has Love?

Readings:
VIGIL: Isa 62:1-5; Acts 13:16-17, 22-25; Matt 1:1-25 or 1:18-25
NIGHT: Isa 9:1-6; Titus 2:11-14; Luke 2:1-14
DAWN: Isa 62:11-12; Titus 3:4-7; Luke 2:15-20
DAY: Isa 52:7-10; Heb 1:1-6; John 1:1-18 or 1:1-5, 9-14

Scripture:
All the ends of the earth have seen the saving power of
   God. (responsorial psalm refrain; cf. Ps 98:3)

Reflection: Have they?
   This psalm verse is a case of typical biblical hyperbole, but it may not be as far from the truth as we think. People everywhere, or nearly everywhere, have seen God's love at work anonymously creating beauty, inspiring know-how for improving life, transforming hearts to love and serve others, and more. But seeing is not necessarily understanding.
   For real understanding, human beings need language above all else. It wasn't by happenstance that God sent the ultimate salvation among us as the *Word* made flesh. Jesus translates God's love into real flesh-and-blood living, working, teaching, healing, reconciling, and seeking out the lost. Words speak loudest and clearest in action. Words and actions together make for the most powerful language.
   And, when it came time for Jesus to speak the ultimate word of love in his death and to walk again among us as the

ultimate word of redemption in the resurrection, God mul-
tiplied the power of the Word by drawing all willing human
beings into the Body of Christ. In one sense, all believers
became fresh words of God, preaching the good news of the
gospel in word and action.

But Caryll Houselander said it more powerfully: "We are
only syllables of the perfect Word." God's one perfect word
has been spoken in Jesus Christ. The word is "love." Every
person who belongs to Christ is, as it were, one syllable of
that word. But, you may say, "love" has only one syllable!
Yes, all the syllables are drawn into that one syllable, legible
in our lives and actions. Christmas is celebrated today, but
the syllables are spoken everywhere, every day, until all the
ends of the earth have seen and learned to understand the
saving power of God.

Meditation: Who has spoken, acted, and lived God's word
of love most powerfully in your life? How have they ex-
pressed it? To whom are you called to speak the same word
of love? How?

Prayer: Jesus Christ, Word of God made flesh, speak your
word of God's love in us and through us. Teach us to hear
it as it is spoken in and through others. Make all of us your
living vocabulary of love.

First Light and Last

Readings: Acts 6:8-10; 7:54-59; Matt 10:17-22

Scripture:
Blessed is he who comes in the name of the LORD:
the LORD is God and has given us light. (Alleluia verse,
    Ps 118:26a, 27a)

Reflection: The first word of creation was "Let there be light" (Gen 1:3). John's gospel, which we heard on Christmas Day, amplifies: "In the beginning was the Word . . . and the Word was God. . . . [T]hrough him was life, and this life was the light of the human race" (John 1:1, 4). Many a Christmas card translates this good news into the picture of a darkened stable bathed in the light from the Child in the manger.

The sight invites us to linger and pray. But only for a while. No one can stay long at the crib.

The shepherds adored and went back to their flocks. The magi worshiped and traveled home to the East. The Holy Family, violently uprooted by an angel in the night, fled to Egypt and never returned to Bethlehem. And we have to go too. In fact, we have to leave sooner than we think. On December 26, St. Stephen breaks unexpectedly into the Christmas story with his witness of courage and death. But as he was dying under a volley of stones, he looked up and saw Jesus bathed in the glory of God, the fiery cloud in which

God appeared throughout the biblical story. So St. Stephen tells us that the light is not only the first word of creation's story but also the last.

Therefore, like the shepherds and the magi, we have to get up from our Christmas worship and travel forward, but we do not leave the light. Indeed, the light travels with us, showing the way. Jesus tells us, "Whoever follows me will not walk in darkness, but will have the light of life" (John 8:12). And that light is available to us every day in the Scriptures: "Your word is a lamp for my feet, / a light for my path" (Ps 119:105). And Jesus, the Light of the World, is the final Word that will be spoken at the path's ending.

No matter how dark the road may sometimes seem, as it must have for St. Stephen's companions in faith, all we have to do is open our eyes and look to see that the light we thought we had left behind in Bethlehem is still shining all around us.

Meditation: Look into the dark corners of your life, and pray to see the light. What does the light show you about Christ's presence in the midst of all your struggles, conflicts, and fears?

Prayer: O Jesus Christ, Light of the World, born for us in Bethlehem and our guide and companion ever since, strengthen our faith to recognize and follow you wherever you lead us, trusting that you will be with us to the end—and beyond.

Page Turner

Readings: 1 John 1:1-4; John 20:1a, 2-8

Scripture:
[W]hat we have seen with our eyes,
what we looked upon
and touched with our hands
concerns the Word of life—
for the life was made visible;
we have seen it and testify to it. (1 John 1:1b-2a)

Reflection: It has happened again. There we were, all settled back into the charming scene at the crib after the trauma of St. Stephen's death. Then someone turned the page once more. Now we're in the tomb, but it's empty. Cloths are strewn around. They remind us of having heard just two days ago about the Mother wrapping her newborn carefully in swaddling clothes to protect him against the night cold. But those clothes had no blood on them. These speak of someone, perhaps even the Mother, wrapping the same Child, now grown to adulthood and crucified, against the cold decay of death. Today, John appears at the tomb with Peter. John never saw the Child born, but he saw the man preach, heal, forgive, and drive out demons. And he saw him die on the cross. But now, now he sees the first evidence that the Crucified has risen from the dead.

"Please, let us go back to the crib and kneel there awhile, won't you?" we ask the page turner. But no. Tomorrow the page will turn again, this time to the bloodbath in Bethlehem, all those children slaughtered. Why this skipping around the story? It's so unsettling!

And so it must be. Shutting ourselves into the comfort of the Christmas story is to miss its point. It belongs to the infancy narratives, which probe the startling reality of the Word of God made human flesh. But the infancy narratives alone are not enough. Precisely because the Word was born in the flesh, he could suffer and die in the flesh on our behalf and rise from the tomb to open for us the door to the eternal light where he now lives in glory.

It is Christ as he is now, crucified, buried, and risen, who keeps turning the pages on us. He wants us to keep remembering the whole story because it is also ours.

Meditation: Early English Christmas carols often wove the wood of the crib into the wood of the cross. Do a little weaving of your own. Think about swaddling clothes, the clothing the soldiers stripped off Jesus and gambled for, the seamless robe, the burial cloths. The story is all of a piece!

Prayer: Lord Jesus Christ, made flesh for us, crucified for us, raised up again for us, walk with us through our whole story, from conception to the place beyond the grave!

Dangerous Child

Readings: 1 John 1:5–2:2; Matt 2:13-18

Scripture:
[Herod] ordered the massacre of all the boys in Bethlehem
and its vicinity
two years old and under. (Matt 2:16)

Reflection: Popular Christmas art can lull us into warm appreciation for the adorable baby in the manger. What could be more helpless and harmless than this pretty little child?

Herod saw the child differently. With a long history of ruthless brutality toward anyone who threatened his royal ambitions, including close family, his immediate reaction to the newborn "king of the Jews" was "Get rid of him!" If that meant children's blood running in the streets, so be it. Compassion toppled thrones. And Herod had no intention of allowing his to fall.

He was right to fear this child, but not for the reasons that unleashed this day's violence. This boy would grow into a man who wore kingship as a scarlet cloak around bleeding shoulders, reminiscent of Bethlehem's slaughtered children, and claim, "My kingdom does not belong to this world" (John 18:36). Nevertheless the once helpless baby Jesus would indeed topple thrones, but thrones that did not belong to this world either, though they held it in thrall with a power Herod could only dream of. Jesus would topple the thrones of sin and death not by more brutality but by taking the place Herod had intended for him among Bethlehem's other murdered children.

Today's feast, horrible in its violence against children, reminds us vividly of the reason the Christ Child came: to save us all, men, women, and children, born and unborn, from the power of the evil held in dread since Eden. And, in contrast with ambitious Herod, he succeeded.

Whether born of our flesh or not, all children are our future. The future always threatens to take the world we have built out of our hands and turn it into something we no longer control. That was what Herod feared. Perhaps it's why we are sometimes tempted to keep children under our thumb one way or another, even to eliminate them as Herod did, to prevent them from changing the future we had counted on. But the future is never in any Herod's hands, or in ours. It is in God's. When we begin to think otherwise, let us remember that one little boy under two years of age escaped the Bethlehem massacre and replaced the reign of death with the reign of everlasting life, all Herods notwithstanding.

Meditation: What reign do we want the world's children to live under—Herod's or Christ's? Many of our choices now, of priorities, relationships, achievements, are our answer. What is yours?

Prayer: God of all times and seasons, turn all our energies to the service of the future you desire as we pray, "Thy kingdom come."

The Constant Future

Readings: 1 John 2:3-11; Luke 2:22-35

Scripture:
"Lord, now let your servant go in peace;
your word has been fulfilled:
my own eyes have seen the salvation
which you prepared in the sight of every people."
   (Luke 2:29-31)

Reflection: Many years ago, in a time of great change, when I asked an older religious sister what she thought should be done, she said to me, "This is not my future, it's yours. Your generation must make the decisions now." The privilege and burden she was laying on my generation left me speechless and humbled.

In today's Gospel, Simeon says it more eloquently. He has longed for the future now laid in his arms as a forty-day-old child. But now he turns to the young mother and lays upon her the burdens she will have to bear to bring this future to maturity.

Today will always be tomorrow's past. Today's lessons are tomorrow's wisdom, forged from a thousand memories, like the ones we have heard about all this season, memories of both fidelity and failure. We have heard about hopes too: hopes for a future that sometimes seemed it could never rise from the ruins wrought by sin. Now as then, the God whose promises have never failed, though human beings have, continues to lay responsibility for the future upon our shoulders as privilege and burden.

The older generation, entrusting its past into the hands of each new generation, like Simeon, always tries to warn us of the swords ahead, lest our courage fail when we come face to face with them. Since most of us don't have Mary's all-embracing faith, we usually don't believe them. But Mary teaches us that both joys and pains will come, woven into the privilege and task entrusted to us. When we falter, as we will, she is always there to pick us up again, dust us off, and set us back on the path, reminding us her son has promised to be with us always while we carry God's gift into our future, and the world's, as she did.

Meditation: Do you remember what your parents tried to tell you to prepare you for the future? How did you react at the time? How did you learn that they had been right after all? What did you do with what you had learned? What do you hope to pass on to those after you?

Prayer: God of past and future, grant us the insight and courage to walk wisely into the future you have entrusted to us through those who have gone before, that we may also leave a legacy of wisdom and hope to the next generation.

Holy Listeners

Readings: Sir 3:2-6, 12-14 or 1 Sam 1:20-22, 24-28; Col 3:12-21 or 3:12-17 or 1 John 3:1-2, 21-24; Luke 2:41-52

Scripture:
After three days they found him in the temple,
sitting in the midst of the teachers,
listening to them. (Luke 2:46)

Reflection: Jesus, God's Word, was born into a family of listeners. Mary and Joseph received the word of his birth with faith, love, and obedience—all essential qualities of the listening heart. And they took the Word into every aspect of their lives. Jesus grew up listening to them and learning from them.

We actually know very little about their family life. Christian imagination often paints idealized pictures of untroubled harmony in home and workshop. Perhaps Christian imagination hasn't paid enough attention to today's gospel.

On a visit to Jerusalem when he was twelve, Jesus was apparently caught in a conflict between the voices that guided his young life. Mary and Joseph probably told him the caravan would leave in the morning, assuming he would come along. But Jesus must have heard a different word from his heavenly Father. So while his parents set off for Nazareth, he went to the temple to sit with the teachers of the Law, apparently without giving a thought to his parents' reactions when they missed him. When they found him, and Mary questioned him sharply, he seems to say they should have understood him better. What the gospel presents as real tensions we should probably not idealize away, lest we lose sight of the human reality of this family because God's saving work unfolds in the context of the human story. Even Jesus was fully human as well as fully divine and had to learn as he grew up, just like any child. Luke confirms it with the final lines of the story: "He went down . . . to Nazareth, / and . . . advanced in wisdom and age and favor."

The picture painted by the Christian imagination fails to tell us that though Jesus, Mary, and Joseph started out as holy individuals, becoming a holy *family* took hard work. Together they had to grow through just such painful experiences as we hear today. In all families, communications are sometimes clumsy. Tensions arise and have to be resolved through listening and understanding that deepen with practice. A *holy* family is a dynamic school of lifelong learning.

Meditation: How have your important relationships been challenged by lack of awareness of others' feelings? How did you work toward more attentive listening, deeper trust, and more honest love?

Prayer: Spirit of God, source of all holiness, teach us to listen, trust, and love more deeply in our closest relationships.

New Year's Resolutions

Readings: 1 John 2:18-21; John 1:1-18

Scripture:
In the beginning was the Word,
and the Word was with God,
and the Word was God. (John 1:1)

Reflection: Tomorrow is New Year's Day. Time for New Year's resolutions!

St. John's gospel opens where the first creation account began: the Word who was with God and who was God. God's Spirit bore that Word into the primal chaos, speaking light, and light shone out. After that, one by one, God's Word drew all of creation out of the waters and into being (Gen 1). John goes on to tell us that "All things came to be through him, / and without him nothing came to be."

Where better to begin our own New Year than with God's creative word? As the first creation unfolded according to God's plan, each new item received three things: a name, a purpose, and a place in the relational scheme of things. For example, two great lights, later named "sun" and "moon," were assigned to govern the day and the night. And of course the culmination of this creative process, set in the magnificent poem of Genesis 1, was human being, male and female, created in God's own image and given the task of continuing God's creative work by peopling the earth and caring for it.

Tomorrow is a bit more modest in scale than the creation of the universe, but we can think about it in the same terms. Before our resolutions hit paper (or computer screen), let's start by asking God to light up the year to come so that we can better see what to do, in what order to do it, and how it fits into the relational scheme of our world. The light, says St. John, is Christ. First on the list, every other item on the list, and the conclusion of the list could very well be lines from the gospels. They set out God's new creation program, speaking the Word into human beings to give new names—"child" instead of "filthy leper," for example; set out new purposes—"Love one another as I have loved you," for example; and new relationships—"You must love the Lord your God with all that's in you and your neighbor as yourself, even your enemies," for example.

Meditation: Tear up your old New Year's resolutions. Take the year that starts tomorrow to the Creator in prayer. Then make that list, including new names—"Mrs. Jones" instead of "that old battle-axe," for example—new purposes—"What can I give" instead of "What can I get," for example—and new relationships, "Hey, old friend, could we put that stupid quarrel behind us and start over again as real friends?," for example. Try it. You might like it. God might too.

Prayer: God, our Creator, teach us to make our life new through your Word this coming year.

A Mother's Blessing

Readings: Num 6:22-27; Gal 4:4-7; Luke 2:16-21

Scripture:
"The LORD bless you and keep you!
The LORD let his face shine upon
you, and be gracious to you!
The LORD look upon you kindly and
give you peace!" (Num 6:24-26)

Reflection: We step into the new calendar year with the blessing of Mary, the Mother of God and our mother, couched in words from the book of Numbers.

Like every mother watching over her children in this violence-ridden world, Mary asks God to give us peace. What she wants for us is her own best Christmas gift: her Son, Jesus Christ, who "is our peace" (Eph 2:14).

Over and over again in the gospels, Jesus greets his troubled disciples with, "Peace be with you." But he warns that he doesn't give peace as the world does, by summit conference and cease-fire agreement and nuclear disarmament, or even by family counseling. His peace is the communion of former enemies in his own Body. It is the fruit of his own self-giving through his words, his works, and finally his death on the cross (see Eph 2:14-18). Peace costs more than words and a handshake, more than psychological growth, more than weapons neutralized. Peace costs love. Peace costs the investment of our own selves. This is Christ's peace. This is the peace Mary asks for us.

In a world darkened by the shadow of sin and death, peace begins with light. In the blessing from Numbers, we remember that Mary gave birth to the One who is not only our peace but also "the light of the world." Through him, we his disciples become bearers of this light: "Live as children of light, for light produces every kind of goodness and righteousness and truth" (Eph 5:8-10). Christ's light enables us to see: to see people beloved by God beneath the skins of hostile neighbors or churlish relatives or angry terrorists; to see ourselves as people who dare to look into our own dark corners with humility and to ask forgiveness of God and others.

What Mary asks for us on this World Day of Peace is a gift that requires our own unremitting work. May God grant us the will and the tools to carry it out!

Meditation: Where are the points of conflict in your own life? Join in Mary's prayer for the light to see truly what you are called to do to work for peace in your own corner of the world.

Prayer: Mary, Mother of God and Queen of peace, pray for us that we may also become a source of Christ's peace for others.

January 2: Saints Basil the Great and Gregory Nazianzen, Bishops and Doctors of the Church

Back to Work!

Readings: 1 John 2:22-28; John 1:19-28

Scripture:
[John] said:
"I am *the voice of one crying out in the desert,*
Make straight the way of the Lord." (John 1:23)

Reflection: We heard John's exhortation before, during Advent, when he and we were looking forward to the coming Messiah. Now that we have celebrated Jesus' birth, isn't John a bit out of date?

Not until Christ has returned in glory. In Advent, we reflected on Christ's once and future coming. Now we are invited to reflect on Christ's present coming. Today is the day many of us have to go back to work. Wherever our workplace is, John might call it the desert.

John's desert isn't the Sahara, with nary a blade of grass to break the white monotony of the dunes. It's a harsh wilderness of rock and shrub that allows no chance of food crops. It's a land where human beings can survive but rarely thrive. Indeed, survival often becomes their only purpose. It was into just such a landscape that John came preparing the way for Christ. It was into that landscape that Jesus came to be baptized, as we shall read in a couple of weeks. It is the place where redemption begins.

Even if our workplace is an oasis in the wilderness, we all have another job to do there, the job given us at our baptism. We have to be "voices" making the landscape less hostile to the coming of Christ, not at Christmas or at the end of time, but right now. Today we remember two saintly thinkers and preachers, Basil the Great and Gregory Nazianzen, who were just such voices at a time when the gospel had slowly begun to break through and still went unheard in many places.

In case you're shaking your head and backing away as you say, "No, no, I'm no preacher, not me!" it might help to remember the advice attributed to St. Francis of Assisi: "Preach the Gospel at all times. When necessary, use words." We are still in the season of rejoicing in the Word of God made flesh in Jesus Christ, who *is* the Good News. The best way to announce his coming here right now is to be ourselves God's good news made flesh. It's not our vocal cords that announce salvation breaking into every desert, it's our lives. It's time to get to work!

Meditation: Think of the people who have been silent Gospel proclamations to you. What caught your attention? Their joy? Their kindness? Their willingness to forgive? Those are sermons worth studying!

Prayer: Lord Jesus Christ, may we know you, love you, and serve you always and everywhere!

Behold the Lamb of God!

Readings: 1 John 2:29-3:6; John 1:29-34

Scripture:
John the Baptist saw Jesus coming toward him and said, "Behold, the Lamb of God, who takes away the sin of the world." (John 1:29)

Reflection: John's words are heard at every Mass when the presider holds up the consecrated Host and says, "Behold the Lamb of God, / behold him who takes away the sins of the world." What are the words doing here in the Christmas season? At Christmas, cute little lambs often appear on Christmas cards in the arms of the shepherds coming to see the newborn savior in the crib, or maybe trailing the Little Drummer Boy. How could such a lamb, even God's Lamb, have anything to do with taking away "the sins of the world," heavy and ugly as it is?

There is a clue in the name "Jesus," which may be commemorated today. In Hebrew, the name means "God helps." In Matthew's gospel, the angel Gabriel instructs Joseph to call Mary's child "Jesus, because he will save his people from their sins" (Matt 1:21). My imagination paints a picture of Jesus grabbing up people and running ahead of the sins that are chasing them rather like wolves in pursuit of sheep.

But the familiar prayer says instead that Jesus saves his people not by snatching them away from their sins but by taking all sin away from them. The picture grows darker here: Jesus carrying a heavy load of all the sin of the world away from pasture and sheepfold to dispose of it in some dark fathomless chasm, like the abyss into which Satan is cast in the book of Revelation. The cross is the image of the burden. The reality is Jesus carrying that load of sin personally into the realm of death where it came from.

This is not a Christmas picture, but it's a picture made possible by Christmas. In fact, it deepens awareness of the saving effect of Christmas, when the Word of God entered into a humanity already marred, torn, and twisted by an immeasurably long history of human sin. Jesus did not sin, but he took up all the consequences of sin and bore them away with him into death.

All the more reason to continue singing "Glory to God" with the Christmas angels!

Meditation: Think about your own experience. Remember how delightful temptation sometimes makes sin appear. Remember the misery that so often follows. Think about Jesus coming along and collecting it from you, a bit like a garbage disposal worker, and taking it away. Remember the freedom then! Consider the sacrament of penance as a way of making the story come true literally.

Prayer: Jesus, Lamb of God, you take away the sins of the world. Please take ours and help us not to go and retrieve them.

Making Connections

Readings: 1 John 3:7-10; John 1:35-42

Scripture:
Andrew, the brother of Simon Peter,
was one of the two who heard John and followed Jesus.
He first found his own brother Simon and told him,
"We have found the Messiah. . . ."
Then he brought him to Jesus. (John 1:40-41)

Reflection: Who brought you?

According to St. John's gospel, connections with Jesus have been forming and growing since John the Baptist saw Jesus passing by and directed two of his disciples, one of them Andrew, toward him. After meeting Jesus in person, Andrew went and got his brother. From then on the pattern was repeated: people whose lives Jesus touched went out and got other people to come along and meet him. Philip fetched Nathanael under his tree; the Samaritan woman went and got her townfolk to see the Messiah.

The popular slogan "Pass it on!" didn't originate in the gospels, but it certainly describes the first Christians—those who met Jesus in person and, later, those who learned of Jesus from others who had, and, still later, others who heard of Jesus from Paul and the other missionaries. Thus grew the powerful network of people Jesus called the kingdom of God. Human beings passing on the Good News to human beings is the basic story of the Body of Christ growing across continents and down through ages.

We haven't yet celebrated the Epiphany, when those three mysterious foreigners discovered the newborn "king of the Jews" and took the news home with them. We haven't yet celebrated the baptism with which the adult Jesus began his own public ministry. We are still in the Christmas season, but the gospels won't let us forget that Christmas itself is God's invitation to "come and see," as Jesus said to Andrew and his friend when they inquired where to find him. From the seed, the tree. From the Christ Child, the whole network of the reign of God. From you and me—what? Who? Where?

Meditation: Today's saint, St. Elizabeth Ann Seton, spread the network of connections to Christ by founding a religious community and the first Catholic school system. We are not all called to such large endeavors, but we are all called to make connections. To return to the opening question: Who brought you to Jesus and to the church? How? Who might you bring? How?

Prayer: Lord Jesus Christ, Word of God made flesh, pour out your Spirit upon us that we might become effective servants of the network that has you for its center.

Come and See!

Readings: 1 John 3:11-21; John 1:43-51

Scripture:
Philip found Nathanael and told him,
"We have found the one about whom Moses wrote in the
    law,
and also the prophets, Jesus, son of Joseph, from Nazareth."
But Nathanael said to him,
"Can anything good come from Nazareth?"
Philip said to him, "Come and see." (John 1:45-46)

Reflection: The proof of the pudding is in the eating, they say, but what if we turn up our nose at the pudding on sight and refuse to take even a tiny bite?

All his public life, Jesus was dismissed out of hand by people who thought they knew who he was and where he came from. Nazareth? That little hole-in-the-wall village? No one important has ever come from there! A carpenter's son? Give me a break!

Quick judgments based on inessentials have undermined many good works and many good workers before they got started. Today's saint, St. John Neumann, might have been one of them had he not, like Jesus, persevered. A Bohemian immigrant with a foreign accent, he arrived in New York a poor man with a dollar in his pocket. He was very short, so people laughed to see him on horseback, visiting his rural parishioners. His clothing was always threadbare because whatever he received, he gave away to someone poorer. But God didn't bother about inessentials, so he became a bishop—and a saint.

Superficial judgments still bar the door when the Gospel comes knocking, and perhaps they always will. Saint John Neumann had to contend with many who dismissed the church as foreign and immigrants as inferior and himself wanting in externals. The phenomenon is hardly confined to the nineteenth century. Place of origin, accent, color, size, IQ scores, and other inessentials continue to hide the real value of many of God's cherished people from those who don't bother to look past their own prejudice. Nathanael is still in good company—though he himself abandoned it.

What changed his mind was Philip's simple invitation: come and see! Nathanael went, looked, saw, and dedicated himself to the unlikely Messiah, the carpenter's son from the hills.

Meditation: If we find ourselves sitting under Nathanael's tree and turning up our noses at the gift offered to us in others because of some superficial criterion they fail to meet, we will be like the ones who refuse the pudding without a taste. Instead, let's listen to Philip. Let's set aside prejudgments and go see and get to know those we've shut out. We might be as surprised as Nathanael at what we find.

Prayer: Jesus, Lord of light, open our eyes to see others as you see them instead of as our biases do.

EPIPHANY AND
BAPTISM OF THE LORD

January 6: The Epiphany of the Lord

Star Struck

Readings: Isa 60:1-6; Eph 3:2-3a, 5-6; Matt 2:1-12

Scripture:
We saw his star at its rising
and have come to do him homage. (Matt 2:2)

Reflection: What star? Speculations abound, scientific and otherwise, but we do know that ancient belief considered a new star the signal of a new king's birth. Did that belief draw the magi to Palestine in quest of the new "king of the Jews"? Too little is known about them for us to say, but Matthew's gospel does say they were "star struck."

Today's English phrase means "captivated by famous people or by fame itself." It dates only to the 1960s, but the magi certainly knew what it meant to be struck, fascinated, and driven by the new star they thought announced the birth of a new king in distant Israel, though no one knows quite why. That experience somehow feels familiar. We also know what it means to be smitten, dazzled, and drawn by an English royal couple or the latest movie "star" without quite being able to explain why. That light stabs and draws us, whether we will it or not.

Perhaps it's because light attracts us toward its source when we ourselves are in the dark, either physically or metaphorically. It offers a focus for wanderers, clarity for the confused, and the unspoken promise of warmth, safety, and company still lodged in a primal memory of huddling together around campfires while predators roamed outside. Wolves and lions no longer walk our streets, but unseen forces greater than ourselves do. And they do not seem to be friendly. Whether you enjoy the wildly popular superhero sagas or laugh them off, they do speak loudly of cultural fears that can no longer be stilled by confidence in a God who surrounds and protects us with guardian angels. Those beliefs have died for many, but the fears have not. Sudden unexplained attacks of violence in what once seemed safe places, like schools, workplaces, and houses of worship, have only stoked those fears.

The birth of the Light of the World, signaled by one singularly bright star traveling ahead to lead seekers to the place, still stirs at least a moment's hope even for many whose religious beliefs are only embers. To believers, it offers the promise of the Savior who came into the frightening darkness of a world ruled by sin and death to carry us into the unquenchable light no darkness can ever again extinguish.

Meditation: Did you or do your children insist on a night-light? What fears sparked it? Why did the light give a sense of safety?

Prayer: O God of light and darkness, send us a star to guide us to the safety you alone can give.

January 7: Monday after Epiphany

Here Comes the Sun!

Readings: 1 John 3:22–4:6; Matt 4:12-17, 23-25

Scripture:
[T]he people who sit in darkness
have seen a great light,
on those dwelling in a land overshadowed by death
light has arisen.
From that time on, Jesus began to preach and say,
"Repent, for the Kingdom of heaven is at hand."
   (Matt 4:16-17)

Reflection: The word "epiphany" means manifestation. On the Solemnity of the Epiphany, we celebrate the manifestation of the Savior, as the Bethlehem angels titled him, to the gentile magi and thus to the world at large. Between the Epiphany and the Baptism of the Lord, we follow unfolding images of who this savior really is, not through abstract theology but through biblical stories of the intersection between Jesus and real life. It becomes a new story of creation.

Once again we remember God's first words: "Let there be light." Today, we hear that new light has risen over a world long darkened by the shadow of sin and death. And the new light is not a planet like the sun but a person: Jesus Christ, Light of the World. For the northern hemisphere, the setting itself speaks: the winter solstice has passed, the hours of darkness diminish, and the hours of daylight begin to grow, but so slowly they only hint at summer to come.

Years ago on a university campus where I worked, the first sun breaking through the long gray of winter caused the campus to blossom with sunbathers clad in as little as possible lying on the grass and soaking up the thin rays. The predominant color was usually a delicate shade of blue because the thermometer didn't play along with the illusion of summer vacation at the beach. Those of us older, colder, and still well wrapped in winter woolens smiled at the sunbathers' folly but couldn't help admiring the strength of their hope as they lived the chilly present as though it were the future summer already come.

And so must we, says Jesus. "Repent!" It sounds gloomy, doesn't it? But Jesus is no sandwich-board prophet warning us to change our evil ways because doom is at hand. Jesus is bringing *good* news: the time has come when we can shed all those winter layers of self-preoccupation that hide our true selves and emerge into the light of the promised sun like those students. We may shiver a bit, others may point fingers and laugh, but we trust that the new Light of the World will show us how to walk in the ways of what Jesus calls "the Kingdom of heaven."

Meditation: Take the risk. Shed a sinful habit or two. Join the sunbathers. Though the calendar says winter, God's love is warmer than you think!

Prayer: Christ, burning sun of God's love, warm our hearts chilled by sin, and free us to live by your light!

Leftovers

Readings: 1 John 4:7-10; Mark 6:34-44

Scripture:
They all ate and were satisfied.
And they picked up twelve wicker baskets full of
    fragments. (Mark 6:44)

Reflection: Yesterday, the Christ made manifest as a child to the magi, was made manifest to the greater world as light.

Today, he is made manifest as the source of bread. There are hints here of the manna God provided the people of Israel in the desert: hungry people in a "deserted place" (Mark 6:32), a prophet, and more than a prophet, to teach them God's word, bread supplied as they need it. But this time the old story is made new.

The people seek Jesus out; they ask for nothing and complain of no one; they are given bread so plentiful that there are ample leftovers. In the old story, manna had to be collected daily, and no leftovers were allowed, except on the Sabbath eve. Now, Jesus seems to have replaced God as the One who gives the bread. What does that suggest about Jesus?

We begin to see Jesus as the human face of God, but it's important to remember that the people of his day, even his disciples, did not yet have the vocabulary to grasp this unheard-of relationship. They were firm monotheists: for them, there was only one God, the God of Israel, the Holy one (see Deut 6:4). This was the faith by which the people defined themselves and to which they adhered forcefully. Instead of speaking about the Trinity, something the church needed centuries to find words for, the evangelists show us something about God by showing us Jesus in action. In John's Gospel, Jesus would state it this way: "Whoever has seen me has seen the Father" (John 14:9).

What do the crowds gathered on the Galilean hillside see? Obviously, they see bread, but perhaps more importantly, they see so much bread that the whole hungry crowd eats its fill, this time with baskets full of leftovers. In seeing Jesus, they see a God who meets their very real needs then gives far more than enough—without demanding anything in return, not even faith in this story.

Meditation: What did you get for Christmas? What did it cost you? What have you done with the leftovers? Too much food? Are the remains in the freezer or on trays at the soup kitchen? Scads of love from family and friends? Is all that love stored away as warm memories, or have you spent some of it on people around you, even strangers? What will others see of God when they look at you and what you do?

Prayer: God of plenty, open our hearts to pour out on others the love you have shown us so abundantly.

January 9: Wednesday after Epiphany

Who Can This Be?

Readings: 1 John 4:11-18; Mark 6:45-52

Scripture:
About the fourth watch of the night,
he came toward them walking on the sea. . . .
He got into the boat with them and the wind died down.
They were completely astounded.
They had not understood the incident of the loaves.
On the contrary, their hearts were hardened.
   (Mark 6:48, 51-52)

Reflection: The picture of who Jesus is gets clearer but not for the poor disciples! In the Old Testament, God is the only one who dominates the seas (e.g. Psalm 107:23-29). And here is Jesus, walking on the waters of the Sea of Galilee in a storm and making the winds die down when he gets into the disciples' boat.

But "their hearts were hardened." Today hard-heartedness usually means lack of kindness or sympathy for others. But here the verse refers to another water story. Psalm 95:8 warns us, "Do not harden your hearts as at Meribah," where God told Moses to strike the rock and bring forth water because the people were convinced they'd die of thirst. Their hard-heartedness was stubborn refusal to imagine God could and would provide for their needs. In that sense, their hard hearts are a hardened imagination that will not envision any outcome except disaster, despite past experience, like the escape from Egypt through parted seas. The hardened heart rejects hope.

The disciples fit this definition. They've just witnessed five thousand people fed with five loaves and two fishes. The allusions to manna in the desert might have given them a hint about what kind of providential power Jesus commanded, but they haven't carried the lesson over. Facing death by drowning, they see Jesus walk up to them across the water and save their lives by calming the winds. In other gospel accounts, they wonder, "What kind of man is this?" The feeding of the crowd and the stilling of the storm could give them a hint, but they refuse to go there. They can't and won't imagine the most obvious answer.

Meditation: Advent, the season of hope, has flowed into Christmas, the season of hope fulfilled and extended into our own future. The question asked us now is, "Who do you say Jesus is? Will you carry the answers of the two seasons over into the present?" How Christ has cared for you in the past? What situations make you fear divine providence will fail you now? Can you imagine Christ's alternatives?

Prayer: Lord Jesus, open our eyes to your care for us, and grant us the grace of hope so that we may always trust in your power and your love for future guidance and protection.

The Face of God

Readings: 1 John 4:19–5:4; Luke 4:14-22a

Scripture:
[Jesus] unrolled the scroll and found the passage where it
   was written:
The Spirit of the Lord . . .
has anointed me
to bring glad tidings to the poor.
He has sent me to proclaim liberty to captives
and recovery of sight to the blind,
to let the oppressed go free . . . . (Luke 4:17-19)

Reflection: On Monday and Wednesday, the gospels suggested that the One made manifest at Epiphany is more than
simply a royal messiah born in David's hometown. They
suggested, in fact, that he was somehow the human face
of the God of Israel, a difficult idea for his first-century
contemporaries. Is that good news or bad? Now as then
some see God as an all-powerful judge who is generally not
pleased with human behavior. Others consider God a
military-style dictator imposing strict laws painfully on us
fallible sinners.

   On Tuesday, when thousands were fed, we began to get a
different picture of what kind of God is walking the land on
human feet: One who uses extraordinary power to feed the

hungry. Today, Jesus names the power at work through him as God's Spirit and spells out what he as Messiah has been sent to do: not judge or enforce laws or run a dictatorship but show mercy toward those who have rarely known mercy: the poor, the captives, the blind, and the oppressed. After that list of sufferers, Jesus hardly needs to say that he brings glad tidings—except of course to the oppressors!

In can be very hard to change our picture of God from someone to be feared or hated to someone to whom we can be quick to open our doors. The Child in the crib is harmless enough, even attractive, but when the Child is made manifest as God's presence, welcome evaporates among many.

Go out and tell it in the highways and byways: whatever you may have feared, God walks among us as mercy, and the news is good!

Meditation: You already knew that. But today invites us all to number the ways in which God's love made visible in Christ has touched our lives with gladness, healing, freedom, and mercy. We members of Christ's Body are now the bearers of that good news to those who are afraid of the judge, the enforcer of laws, or the dictator.

Prayer: O Mercy of God, come among us in human flesh, inflame us with gratitude for your gifts to us, and teach us how to spread the Good News to those who expect a different God.

January 11: Friday after Epiphany

Gladly!

Readings: 1 John 5:5-13; Luke 5:12-16

Scripture:
[The leper] pleaded with [Jesus], and said,
"Lord, if you wish, you can make me clean."
Jesus stretched out his hand, touched him, and said,
"I do will it. Be made clean." (Luke 5:12-13)

Reflection: Yesterday we heard a list of the kinds of mercy Jesus came to bring as the Messiah who was so much more than anyone expected. Today we read a touching story of that mercy at work. Yesterday's list of mercy's designated recipients made no demand on the Giver, except time and whatever effort the Spirit required. Today's story is different.

Chances are that you and I will never meet a leper like the one Jesus healed. The last two leper colonies in the United States, in Carville, Louisiana, and on the island of Molokai, were closed some time ago as medical advances rendered them unnecessary. Hansen's disease, as leprosy is now known, is a bacterial infection that can be cured with drugs distributed free of charge by the World Health Organization in those parts of the world where it still exists, especially among the poor. It isn't actually highly contagious, but it has always been highly feared.

In Jesus' day, however, leprosy, which included both Hansen's disease and other skin diseases, had no cure. As all gospel readers know, lepers were therefore strictly isolated physically and socially. It was widely believed that the disease could be transmitted through simple touch. So most people wisely fled at the sound of the leper's bell or cry of "Unclean!" Jesus didn't. Instead, he reached out to the leper and touched him. And gladly, it seems, from his first response to the leper's trusting plea.

Jesus teaches us that God's love knows no fear. God's love avoids no one. Absolutely no one. The cure of the leper is the most dramatic example of a messiah who not only heals the helpless but also dines with enemies and, in fact, wades into the very depths of death to bring out those trapped there. And does so gladly! (See Heb 12:2.)

Meditation: Christ never begrudges love to anyone, no matter how unappealing, demanding, and ungrateful they may be. Think about some of the people you have brushed off or turned away because you found them repellant or demanding. Perhaps they whined or presumed or took advantage of you or made no return on your good will. Whatever happened to Jesus' love, given gladly even to a leper? Remember what he said: whatever you did to these, the least (including the least appealing), you, in fact, did to him (see Matt 25:40). His is indeed saving love: he saves us from our worst selves in order to make us our best selves!

Prayer: Jesus Christ, Savior, teach us to love gladly as you have loved us!

January 12: Saturday after Epiphany

Here Comes the . . . Bridegroom?

Readings: 1 John 5:14-21; John 3:22-30

Scripture:
The one who has the bride is the bridegroom;
the best man, who stands and listens for him,
rejoices greatly at the bridegroom's voice. (John 3:29)

Reflection: In denying that he is the Messiah, John the Baptist uses what might seem to us an odd image: he calls himself the best man at the upcoming wedding when the Messiah will take his place as bridegroom.

The image of the Messiah-Bridegroom would have seemed not odd but scandalous to John's hearers. They would have been familiar with the long love story told in the Old Testament, where God is the Bridegroom and Israel is the chosen bride, not noted for being faithful. Once again, then, today's gospel is hinting and more than hinting at the shocking, inexplicable idea that Jesus, the flesh-and-blood Jesus the Baptist has already met, is somehow identified with God. "No, no, no, this cannot be," John's hearers would have said in horror.

Believing what we believe, that the Child whose birth we just celebrated less than three weeks ago is indeed the Son of God in the flesh, we don't find the image horrifying, only puzzling. Since we know from the rest of the gospel story that Jesus never married, we're left with a string of questions:

"Who is the bride? When is the wedding? Are we invited?" The Old Testament tradition has already given us a clue about the bride: "she" is God's people, now including us, so, yes, we will be at the wedding (unless we choose to drop out of God's people).

The "when" is a bit more slippery. The post-Christmas liturgy, especially the Liturgy of the Hours, holds that the "wedding" between the Word of God and humanity took place at Jesus' conception. The book of Revelation places it at the very end of the human story when Christ, the Lamb who was slain, takes as bride the new Jerusalem, that is, God's redeemed people and final dwelling place.

The slipperiness is a useful clue, in our more gender-aware society, that the envisioned God-human "marriage" is not a gender-based physical relationship. It is the astonishing covenant bond between God and humanity finally and profoundly realized in the incarnation, where divinity and humanity are forever conjoined. (Remember: for the Israelites who first used the imagery, God had neither body nor gender, and the bridal people included both men and women.) It utterly transcends our experience and therefore our language.

Meditation: How do you live the reality of communion with God and others in the Body of Christ? How does it affect interactions with others? How does it affect prayer?

Prayer: God of love and fidelity, draw us to yourself in Christ that we may grow into that communion in our everyday life.

Time to Go!

Readings: Isa 42:1-4, 6-7 or Isa 40:1-5, 9-11; Acts 10:34-38 or Titus 2:11-14; 3:4-7; Luke 3:15-16, 21-22

Scripture:
. . . the Holy Spirit descended upon [Jesus]. . . .
And a voice came from heaven,
"You are my beloved Son;
with you I am well pleased." (Luke 3:21-22)

Reflection: The past week has already woven together Old and New Testament stories and images to show Jesus as the human face of God at work in the world. Today's gospel states in no uncertain terms that God, both Father and Spirit, claims Jesus as the Son.

This claim isn't an invitation to Jesus' contemporaries or today's readers to fall down in adoration and stay there. Adoration is certainly important, but today's feast celebrates Jesus' public baptismal send-off into a wider world to do God's work.

What is the work? Last Monday's gospel summarized it succinctly: Jesus came to proclaim that the kingdom of God is at hand. And it wasn't the kingdom expected by those who anticipated a political messiah come to restore the Davidic kingdom to its former glory. God's reign is better described as the original web of harmonious relationships badly torn in Eden. So Jesus preached a renewed life-giving way for people to relate to one another: reverence, love, and service, instead of rejection of undesirables, feuds with enemies, and competition for goods. And he performed astonishing signs to show what he meant: the hungry fed in plenty, lepers healed and reunited with their communities, tax collectors invited to table. And, being who he was, he revealed God working through and beyond human interactions: incurable illnesses healed, sinners forgiven, and even the dead raised.

If we ourselves are baptized, this feast also renews our own send-off to do God's work in and with Christ: to proclaim and live God's reign in the flesh, mending the threads of the torn web.

Meditation: How? God has given us the gift of creativity, so let's think and act creatively—and humbly, lest, having bitten off more than we can chew, we give it all up and go home in despair. Let's start with calling alienated relatives, not peace conferences; speaking respectfully to neighbors with different accents, not resolving the whole immigration crisis today; putting away hurtful words, not destroying all weapons of violence by Tuesday. If we all paint in small strokes with the brushes and colors we've been given, God can finish the big picture.

Tomorrow is Monday. Time to get going!

Prayer: O God, you make all things new in Christ. Pour out your Spirit upon us so that we may take our assigned places and persevere in your work.

References

December 7: Saint Ambrose, Bishop and Doctor of the Church
The prayer is paraphrased from St. Richard, bishop of Chichester
(1197–1253).

December 14: Saint John of the Cross
Rule of St. Benedict, Prologue 1. There are many editions of
St. Benedict's rule. One easily accessible online is at: http:
//www.osb.org/rb/text/toc.html.
Henry David Thoreau (1817–62), *Walden*, http://www.literature
page.com/read/walden.html.

December 25: The Nativity of the Lord
Quoted in Maisie Ward, *Caryll Houselander: That Divine Eccentric*
(New York: Sheed and Ward, 1962), 136.